Original title:
Love, Unfiltered

Copyright © 2024 Swan Charm
All rights reserved.

Author: Daisy Dewi
ISBN HARDBACK: 978-9916-79-212-4
ISBN PAPERBACK: 978-9916-79-213-1
ISBN EBOOK: 978-9916-79-214-8

Ethereal Union of Spirits

In silent whispers, souls unite,
A bond of grace, shining bright.
Transcendent love, a sacred hymn,
Guided by light, a realm within.

Through trials faced, hand in hand,
We rise together, strong we stand.
In the embrace of the divine,
Our spirits dance, forever entwined.

The Book of Heartfelt Connections

In pages worn, the stories dwell,
Of love and faith, we weave our spell.
Each line a testament, a prayer,
Binding our hearts in tender care.

With every word, a sacred vow,
Our path unfolds, as time allows.
In the quiet moments, we find grace,
A tapestry of love, we embrace.

A Psalm for Two

Together we sing, in harmony,
Our voices rise, a melody.
In every note, a cherished dream,
Bound by faith, like a river's stream.

Through the valleys, we walk as one,
Beneath the stars, 'til day is done.
A song of hope that never fades,
In love's embrace, our spirit wades.

Beneath the Canopy of Affection

Under the boughs of love's embrace,
We gather strength, we find our place.
In gentle shadows, whispers flow,
A sacred bond, the heart will grow.

With every breeze, our spirits soar,
In this haven, we seek no more.
A sanctuary, forever true,
Beneath this canopy, me and you.

Sacred Communion of Two

In silence deep, where two hearts pray,
A sacred bond, they find their way.
Through whispered hopes and gentle grace,
Together they seek a holy place.

In every glance, a world is spun,
A dance of light, where love has won.
Hand in hand, they rise above,
In unity, they breathe in love.

Elysian Threads of Connection

Threads of light weave through the night,
Binding souls in soft twilight.
Each heartbeat hums a sacred tune,
Illuminating the path to the divine moon.

In gentle touch, the spirit sings,
Unveiling the joy that such love brings.
With every prayer, their spirits soar,
Connected forever, they seek no more.

The Spirit's Tender Covenant

In sacred vows, their hearts align,
A covenant forged by love divine.
Through trials faced and joys embraced,
Their spirits merge, in faith interlaced.

With every promise, truth is spoken,
A bond so strong, shall not be broken.
In the quiet, their souls ignite,
A testament to love's pure light.

Revelations of the Joined Heart

In union found, a secret shared,
A revelation, of love declared.
Each moment breathes the sacred grace,
Of two who journey, face to face.

With open arms, they embrace the flow,
As wisdom blooms from seeds they sow.
In the silence, their spirits meet,
In the joined heart, lies love complete.

Holy Threads of Affection

In the quiet prayer of night,
Hearts entwined in sacred light.
Whispers of love softly soar,
Binding souls forevermore.

With every tear that falls in grace,
Gentle hands in warm embrace.
Threads of kindness weave a chain,
In unity, we share the pain.

Through storms of doubt, we stand as one,
Under the gaze of the risen sun.
Faithful hearts, a guiding star,
Drawing us close, no matter how far.

In the tapestry of life, we find,
Colors of hope, compassion blind.
Holy threads of love now spun,
Together, forever, we are one.

Celestial Bonds of Yearning

In the heavens, souls unite,
Bound by whispers of the light.
Yearning hearts in sacred plea,
Celestial love shall set us free.

Across the valleys, deep and wide,
In faith, we'll walk, together stride.
Through shadows cast, we will not fear,
For in His grace, we draw near.

The stars above, a witness true,
To the love that blooms anew.
In each heartbeat, sacred song,
Celestial bonds that keep us strong.

Through layers of doubt, we shall rise,
In the embrace of endless skies.
Our spirits dance, a vibrant flame,
Yearning hearts, calling His name.

The Gospel of Connection

In the scripture of our hearts,
Connection forms as life imparts.
With every verse, we find our way,
The gospel shared in love each day.

Through trials faced, we grow in trust,
In faith and grace, we find the just.
The words of past guide our soul,
Building bridges, making whole.

Voices rise in harmony,
A hymn of hope, our destiny.
Together strong, we seek the light,
In every shadow, stand upright.

From lips of wisdom, truth is told,
Connection deep, a love of gold.
With open hearts and humble mind,
The gospel of connection designed.

Graceful Ties that Bind

Threads of mercy, woven tight,
Graceful ties, they shine so bright.
In every heart, a gentle tie,
Connecting souls as years go by.

Through trials faced and burdens shared,
In silent moments, we have cared.
Our paths unite, like rivers flow,
Unity in love, we sow.

With every prayer, a bond is formed,
In storms of life, we stay warm.
Hand in hand, we walk the way,
Graceful ties that ever stay.

In the light of dawn, we rise,
Guided by our sacred ties.
Together in His presence, find,
The grace and love that binds mankind.

Pilgrims of the Heart's Desires

In search of grace we tread the way,
With whispered hopes that gently sway.
Our footsteps guided by the light,
That dances softly through the night.

Each yearning soul, a sacred flame,
In unity, we call His name.
Through trials faced, our spirits rise,
Embracing love that never dies.

With every prayer, our bonds grow strong,
In harmony, we sing our song.
Together on this path we roam,
Our hearts forever seeking home.

A journey woven with His grace,
With every tear, we find our place.
For in our quests, the truth we find,
That love alone can heal the blind.

Signs of the Seraphic Bond

In every smile, a sign divine,
The seraphs trace the love we find.
With wings of hope, they lift us high,
Connecting hearts beneath the sky.

Through silent prayers, our spirits soar,
Together, we unlock Heaven's door.
In every touch, a sacred spark,
Illuminating shadows dark.

The laughter shared, a holy gift,
As hearts entwine, our spirits lift.
With every step, we walk the line,
Where faith and love in unity shine.

In trials faced, a bond we share,
The seraphs whisper in the air.
With every joy and every sigh,
Our hearts become the reason why.

A Testament of Embodied Trust

In every glance, we share a vow,
A testament to here and now.
With open hearts, we dare to see,
The sacred truth of you and me.

Through every storm, our hands entwine,
In faith we stand, our spirits shine.
With every promise, we evoke,
A deeper bond that time has spoke.

The whispers soft, the silence loud,
In trust we stand, a faithful crowd.
Through trials faced, our roots grow deep,
In love's embrace, we learn to leap.

With each new day, our spirits sing,
In wisdom found, we take to wing.
A testament to love's true art,
As one we soar, no soul apart.

Notes from the Holiest Union

In sacred spaces, love's refrain,
The notes of faith in heart remain.
With every breath, a harmony,
From depths of soul, eternally.

Through sacred bonds, the music flows,
A symphony that only grows.
In unity, we find our song,
Resounding deep where we belong.

Each note a prayer, each chord a hope,
A melody in which we cope.
Through trials faced, our voices rise,
In love's embrace, a sweet surprise.

The holiest union, pure and bright,
Guiding us through the darkest night.
With every heartbeat, pure as gold,
The notes of love, forever told.

The Height of Sacred Connection

In whispers soft, the Spirit calls,
A gentle breeze through sacred halls.
Hearts entwined in faith's embrace,
We journey forth, a holy grace.

Each prayer a bridge to realms above,
Where mercy flows, and purest love.
With every step, we seek the light,
In unity, our souls take flight.

Through trials faced, we rise anew,
In darkest times, His presence true.
The stars align, the heavens sing,
In gratitude, our praises spring.

Together bonded, hand in hand,
We walk this path, a promised land.
The sacred bond, our guiding star,
In faith's embrace, we wander far.

So let us rise, our voices clear,
In every heart, the love draw near.
For in this space where spirits blend,
We find the strength that will not end.

Chronicles of the Affectionate

In pages worn, the stories dwell,
Of love divine, we have to tell.
With open hearts, we share the truth,
A timeless bond, the spirit's youth.

As kindness flows through every deed,
In moments shared, our hearts we lead.
Each chapter speaks of grace bestowed,
In gentle acts, our love bestowed.

Through trials faced, we stand as one,
In every tear, the race we run.
With joyful hearts, we celebrate,
In faith, our bonds, we elevate.

The whispers soft of sacred praise,
In every word, our hearts ablaze.
Together strong, we share the tale,
Of love's embrace that will not fail.

So join the chorus, let it rise,
In harmony, our spirits fly.
In sacred stories, we believe,
With every breath, our hearts reprieve.

Unfurling the Divine Design

In every leaf that sways and drifts,
A sacred touch, the Spirit lifts.
The beauty vast that we behold,
In nature's arms, His love unfolds.

With every dawn, the sun shall rise,
Illuminating the endless skies.
In tranquil streams where waters flow,
The signs of love, we come to know.

Through seasons change, our hearts remain,
In joy and sorrow, love's refrain.
Each moment spent, a gift divine,
In gratitude, our souls entwine.

The universe, a grand display,
Of dreams and hopes, a blessed way.
A tapestry of faith and grace,
In every thread, His warm embrace.

So let us walk this path of light,
Embracing all with love's delight.
For in this life, the design shows,
In every heart, the Spirit glows.

Mapping Sacred Journeys

With map in hand, we seek the way,
Through valleys deep, to bright array.
In footsteps soft, the journey starts,
Each point aligned, our sacred hearts.

Through mountains high, and rivers wide,
In faith, we navigate the tide.
With every twist, and every turn,
The light of truth begins to burn.

Across the fields, in morning dew,
The signs we see, a love so true.
As shadows fall, we share the song,
In unity, we all belong.

The compass set, our spirits bold,
With every tale, a truth unfolds.
In every step, the promise near,
A sacred path, we hold so dear.

So let us find what's yet to be,
In every heart, divinity.
Through sacred journeys, side by side,
We map the love that will not hide.

Divine Whispers of the Heart

In the silence where shadows lie,
Hearts entwined in a sacred sigh,
Soft murmurs dance on the breeze,
Calling forth love, a gentle tease.

In evening's glow, the spirit sings,
A melody of celestial things,
Each note a whisper, pure and bright,
Guiding the lost toward the light.

In prayer's embrace, souls ignite,
Filling the void with holy insight,
Together we strive, united and bold,
In the warmth of grace, our stories unfold.

Through trials faced and burdens shared,
Divine presence always cared,
With faith as our anchor, we rise above,
Cradled forever in unconditional love.

To the heavens, our voices soar,
As we seek to connect, forevermore,
With every heartbeat, the truth we see,
In divine whispers, we find our decree.

Sacred Echoes of Tenderness

In the garden where kindness blooms,
Rays of love dispel all glooms,
Gentle hands, a warm embrace,
Whispering peace in a sacred space.

In soft raindrops, compassion flows,
Nurturing hearts, where mercy grows,
Kindred spirits celebrate the light,
As tender echoes banish the night.

In moments shared and laughter's song,
We find our place where we belong,
Hearts resonate in divine refrain,
A symphony of joy, free of disdain.

In trials endured with grace and care,
Love's resilience, a potent prayer,
We rise as one, holding hands tight,
In sacred echoes, we find our might.

In the stillness, let silence speak,
Of bonds unbroken, of the meek,
With each heartbeat, may we treasure this,
The sacred echoes of tender bliss.

The Sanctity of Embraced Souls

In the warmth of the morning light,
Two souls dance in sacred sight,
A gentle touch ignites the flame,
In the heart's embrace, love's eternal name.

With every breath, a promise made,
In harmony, fears start to fade,
Together they walk, hand in hand,
Guided by grace, in love they stand.

Through storms that shake and winds that moan,
Their bond grows deeper, never alone,
In solace found within the night,
The sanctity of love feels so right.

In whispered prayers, they rise and fall,
The essence of truth, they heed the call,
In moments cherished, they find their goal,
In the unity of embraced souls.

Through paths unseen, their journey unfolds,
In the tapestry of life, their story told,
With every heartbeat, side by side,
In the sanctity of love, forever abide.

Cherished Flames of Belonging

In the hearth where love resides,
Cherished flames, where hope abides,
Flickering brightly, casting light,
In the shadows of the night.

With open arms and hearts aligned,
In every moment, love defined,
Together as one, a sacred song,
Weaving a bond where we belong.

In each embrace, a promise shines,
As the universe in us entwines,
Through trials faced, we find our way,
Cherished flames will never sway.

In laughter shared and tears we mend,
The warmth of kinship, love transcends,
In the tapestry of life, threads combine,
In cherished flames, our spirits shine.

With every flicker, a prayer we send,
In the glow of connection, hearts unbend,
Together we rise, as night turns to dawn,
In cherished flames, our love lives on.

Grace in Every Glance

In the silence of the dawn, we find,
Soft whispers from the sacred wind.
Each glance a blessing, divinely entwined,
A gentle touch where love begins.

The sunlight dances on leaves so green,
Nature's hymn, a spiritual call.
In every moment, the presence seen,
Grace abounding, we rise and fall.

Through trials faced and shadows cast,
Hope ignites in the darkest night.
With every breath, the love holds fast,
Guiding souls into the light.

Faith blooms brightly like flowers rare,
In the heart's garden, alive and pure.
Together, we gather strength in prayer,
In love's embrace, we find our cure.

With gratitude, we lift our eyes,
To the heavens where blessings flow.
In every glance, a sacred prize,
In grace, we learn, we heal, we grow.

Illuminated Passions of the Heart

In the shadows of the night, we tread,
With lanterns of faith held high above.
Illuminated whispers, softly said,
Reveal the depths of a boundless love.

Hearts ignited by divine desire,
Flickering flames of hope and might.
Passions burning like unquenchable fire,
In the stillness, we find our light.

Every moment a canvas of grace,
Brushstrokes of mercy paint our souls.
In the sacred reverence of this place,
Love's pure essence, our spirit consoles.

Together we dance in rhythmic embrace,
Unfurled like wings of an angel's flight.
Hearts entwined by a heavenly trace,
In the harmony of love's delight.

These passions, bold and beautifully bright,
Guide us along the sacred path.
In the embrace of love's soft light,
We find our peace, we know no wrath.

Divine Rhythms of Affection

In the stillness of a sacred space,
Where whispers echo through the air,
Divine rhythms awaken grace,
We find love's pulse in heartfelt prayer.

With each heartbeat, a song of hope,
A melody that softly sways.
Through trials faced, we learn to cope,
In the embrace of love always.

The beauty of creation sings,
In every soul a spark of light.
With love, our spirit freely springs,
Illuminating the darkest night.

As hands unite in common quest,
Sharing dreams and burdens near.
Divine affection brings us rest,
In the arms of love, we persevere.

Together risen, we stand so tall,
In unity, we find our way.
The divine whispers, a loving call,
In rhythms of affection, we stay.

Sacred Embrace of Souls

In the quietude of a tender grace,
Two souls meet in the sacred night.
A warm embrace, a holy space,
Bound together by love's pure light.

Every heartbeat echoes the truth,
In communion, we find our song.
The joy of innocence, the wisdom of youth,
In love's sanctuary, we belong.

With eyes that see beyond the veil,
Together we journey through time and fate.
In the dance of life, we shall prevail,
In the arms of love, we celebrate.

Beneath the starlit sky, we pray,
For peace to reign in every heart.
In the sacred embrace, we find our way,
A tapestry of souls, never apart.

As the sun sets and shadows merge,
With faith, we rise to greet the dawn.
In love's embrace, we feel the urge,
To live as one, forever drawn.

Miracles Found in Touch

In gentle hands, the blessings flow,
A soothing balm, a healing glow.
With every touch, the spirit sings,
A sacred bond that love now brings.

When hearts collide in tender grace,
A miracle reflects its face.
Through shared embraces, pain will fade,
In unity, our faith is made.

The warmth ignites, the darkness clears,
In silent whispers, calm our fears.
With every caress, hope ignites,
In touch divine, our souls take flight.

Divine embrace, where blessings meet,
In every heartbeat, love's retreat.
A tapestry of grace unwinds,
In every touch, God's love we find.

With joyful hearts, we now receive,
The gift of touch, we do believe.
In every moment, sacred trust,
Miracles bloom like golden dust.

The Sacred Garden of Affection

In every petal, love is found,
In fragrant blooms, our hearts abound.
The sacred garden, lush with grace,
Where every soul can find its place.

With gentle hands, we tend the earth,
In every breath, we find our worth.
In sunlight's kiss and evening dew,
Affection grows, both pure and true.

The blossoms cheer, their colors bright,
In every hue, a sweet delight.
A sanctuary, soft and warm,
Where love protects us from all harm.

In whispered prayers beneath the trees,
We find our solace in the breeze.
The sacred garden knows our fears,
And nurtures hope through all the years.

With every blossom, joy begets,
In sacred ties, our spirit sets.
The garden thrives, in love's embrace,
In nature's heart, we find our grace.

Emblems of Covenant Kindness

In every act of kindness shown,
A bond of love, forever grown.
Each gentle word, a promise made,
In covenant, we shall not fade.

With open hearts, we share our days,
In humble service, love displays.
Emblems of grace in every deed,
A tranquil heart fulfills the need.

Through trials faced, we stand as one,
A shining light, beneath the sun.
In every gesture, kindness shared,
In God's embrace, we feel prepared.

Covenant whispers softly call,
In cherished moments, we find all.
We lift each other, spirits raised,
In love profound, we are amazed.

A sacred bond, forever true,
In every act, we renew.
Emblems of kindness fill our soul,
In unity, we are made whole.

Prayers Wrapped in Embrace

In every hug, a prayer takes flight,
A quiet moment, pure delight.
Wrapped in warmth, our spirits blend,
In love's embrace, we find our mend.

Through trials faced, we hold on tight,
In each other's arms, we find the light.
A whispered prayer, a soft caress,
In unity, we feel the blessedness.

With gentle hearts, we seek the divine,
In every touch, the stars align.
Prayers woven in tender care,
In love's embrace, we lay our bare.

Each heartbeat echoes hopes anew,
In shared affection, love breaks through.
Wrapped in kindness, we shall rise,
In prayer's embrace, our spirits fly.

Together we stand, hand in hand,
In faith and trust, on sacred land.
With every hug, our souls ignite,
In love's embrace, we find our light.

Reverent Echoes of Amity

In shadows deep, we find our light,
Together we rise, casting out fright.
Voices unite in sacred song,
Harmony whispers, where hearts belong.

Hands intertwined, we seek the grace,
In every smile, love we embrace.
Threads of compassion weave our fate,
In this bond, we rejuvenate.

Steps of kindness mark our path,
In moments shared, we conquer wrath.
With faith as our guide, we boldly tread,
In the tapestry of love, we are spread.

Let not darkness dim our view,
For each heartbeat brings life anew.
With reverence, we sing our prayer,
In echoes of joy, we are laid bare.

Seraphic Moments of Togetherness

Upon the dawn, we share our dreams,
In whispered hopes, a radiant beam.
Each moment cherished, pure and bright,
Together as one, we reach the light.

In laughter's echo, our spirits soar,
In unity's embrace, we long for more.
A tapestry woven with threads divine,
In this sacred space, our hearts align.

As stars above, we guide each other,
In trials faced, we are like no other.
In tender silence, we grasp the truth,
Together we blossom, eternal youth.

With seraphic grace, we hold the day,
In each shared moment, we find our way.
A bond unbroken, forever we stand,
In the sacred circle, hand in hand.

Heartfelt Pilgrimage of Unity

With humble hearts, we seek the path,
In journeying forth, we escape the wrath.
Each footstep whispers tales of old,
In unity's warmth, our spirits bold.

Through valleys low and mountains high,
Together we tread, beneath the sky.
In every challenge, our faith we share,
With love as our compass, we shall declare.

In moments lovely, we find our song,
In grateful hearts, we all belong.
With kindness as fuel, our spirits ignite,
In this heartfelt pilgrimage, we find light.

Together we stand, side by side,
In devotion's embrace, we shall abide.
A tapestry woven with love and trust,
In unity's cradle, together we'll thrust.

Transcendent Journeys of Together

In the stillness, our souls entwine,
Through each encounter, the divine.
Transcendence calls in every sigh,
As we navigate the endless sky.

With every heartbeat, time stands still,
In shared resilience, we find our will.
With eyes alight, we embrace the dawn,
Together we journey, forever drawn.

In sacred moments, we rise and shine,
Reflecting grace in the divine design.
With arms wide open, we cast aside
The doubts that linger, the fears that bide.

Every chapter penned in love's soft hue,
In transcendent journeys, we find what's true.
With every step, our spirits soar high,
Together we flourish, eternally nigh.

The Sanctuary of Shared Souls

In the heart where spirits meet,
Whispers of love and grace compete.
Harmony in faithful embrace,
Together we find our rightful place.

In stillness, our voices rise,
Echoing truths that never die.
In unity, our journeys blend,
A sacred bond that shall not end.

In prayer, we gather as one,
Beneath the warmth of the sacred sun.
Each soul a light, shining bright,
Guiding each other through the night.

With hands held tight and hearts aglow,
We navigate paths where rivers flow.
The sanctuary of shared souls,
Where love's sweet melody consoles.

In whispers soft, we share our dreams,
In silence, the truth gently beams.
Together we rise, never to fall,
In the sanctuary, we welcome all.

Transcendent Affinity in Silence

In the still, where spirits dwell,
Silence speaks, a sacred bell.
Each moment breathes a subtle grace,
Transcendent affinity we embrace.

Through love's lens, we truly see,
The hidden threads of unity.
In quietude, our hearts align,
A bond that glows, divine and fine.

In the depths of serene night,
We find our way, through shadows, light.
Whispers of the heavens near,
In silence, all we hold is clear.

A symphony of heartbeats played,
The sacred dance of love displayed.
As we journey, dreams entwine,
In the silence, your heart is mine.

Together we walk this sacred ground,
In every breath, a song profound.
Transcendence grows, a soft embrace,
In silence, we find our holy space.

The Prayer for Togetherness

In the glow of morning rays,
We bow our heads in earnest praise.
A prayer for love to guide our way,
To intertwine our hearts today.

With every word, a wish is cast,
In unity, our hope stands fast.
Embracing differences, vast and wide,
In love's embrace, we shall abide.

Through trials faced and sorrows shared,
With gentle hands, we show we cared.
A prayer, a bond, a sacred vow,
Together, we flourish in the now.

Let kindness flow through every space,
Glimmers of light in love's embrace.
In the prayer for togetherness,
We find a strength that knows no stress.

With hearts aligned, we lift our voice,
Together in faith, we rejoice.
The world transforms in love's sweet song,
In this prayer, we all belong.

Flames of Divine Yearning

In the night, the flames do rise,
Burning bright before the skies.
A yearning deep that won't subside,
In the sacred light, we confide.

Each flicker tells a timeless tale,
Of dreams ignited, spirits sail.
Together, hearts ablaze we stand,
In the warmth of the divine command.

The blaze, it dances, a mystic call,
With flames of love, we encompass all.
In unity, we seek the light,
Guiding each other through the night.

With every prayer, the fire grows,
In divine yearning, wisdom flows.
In the warmth of faith, we find our way,
Holding tight to hope each day.

Flames of love, pure and bright,
In these embers, we take flight.
Together we rise, forever strong,
In the blaze of love, we belong.

Anointed by Emotion

In shadows deep, the spirit weeps,
A whisper calls, our longing keeps.
With hearts ablaze, in fervent prayer,
We seek the light, beyond despair.

Through trials faced, our faith ignites,
Beneath the stars, eternal sights.
In moments spent, we feel the grace,
Together bound, in time and space.

For love divine, in every tear,
Anointed souls, forever near.
With every breath, a sacred token,
In unity, our hearts unbroken.

We rise anew, from ashes cold,
With courage strong, and spirits bold.
In sacred hymns, our voices blend,
The journey shared, with Love, we mend.

To light the path, our spirits soar,
In each embrace, we seek for more.
Anointed by emotion true,
In faith, we live, in love we grew.

The Covenant of Togetherness

In hands entwined, we make our vow,
A sacred bond, we honor now.
Through trials fierce and joys we share,
In faith, united, we declare.

For every smile, each tear we've shed,
The love we give, from hearts widespread.
In silent nights, our whispers flow,
A covenant that time will know.

In laughter bright, in sorrows deep,
A promise made, our souls we keep.
Through every storm, together stand,
In grace embraced, we are a band.

With sacred strength, our spirits rise,
Beneath the stars, and endless skies.
Together bound, we face the dawn,
In love's embrace, we carry on.

In faith we walk, hand in hand,
With every step, a holy land.
The covenant stands, forever true,
In each heartbeat, I find you.

Holy Revelations of Desire

In quiet prayer, desires bloom,
With every wish, dispelling gloom.
In sacred dreams, our hearts align,
A glimpse of love, the pure divine.

With passion's fire, our spirits dance,
In every glance, a fleeting chance.
Through whispered words, we seek the light,
In holy reverence, hearts take flight.

For in the depths, where love resides,
Revelations speak, where truth abides.
In sacred spaces, souls entwined,
Desires known, and paths designed.

In moments shared, where time stands still,
Yearning hearts, with fervent will.
A holy bond, forever blessed,
In love's embrace, our souls find rest.

With every dawn, our spirits rise,
In holy light, under vast skies.
The revelations guide our way,
In love we trust, come what may.

Testament of Sacred Moments

In stillness found, the sacred pause,
Moments shared, bring forth applause.
Each heartbeat echoes in the night,
A testament of love's pure light.

With every glance, the world fades away,
In holy silence, our spirits sway.
In laughter's ring, or tear's soft fall,
We cherish the gift of it all.

Through valleys low and mountains high,
The moments crafted never die.
In sacred time, our stories weave,
A tapestry of love, we believe.

In gentle hands, trust softly grows,
A testament of all we chose.
With faith as our guide, we'll journey on,
In every sunset, a new dawn.

Eternal bonds in every embrace,
We find our peace in time and space.
The sacred moments shape our hearts,
In love's sweet song, a life imparts.

Chants of the Cherished

In the quiet night, we gather,
Voices raised to heights untold.
Each whisper a flame, a beacon,
In unity, our spirits hold.

Beneath the stars, our hearts entwine,
A tapestry of grace we weave.
With sacred words, we seek the divine,
In love, we truly believe.

Through trials faced, hand in hand,
We find our strength in prayer's embrace.
Together we stand, in this sacred land,
Finding solace in the grace.

Oh, cherished moments, we revere,
With every breath, our souls ignite.
In harmony, we cast out fear,
Our spirits soaring, pure delight.

As dawn breaks forth, a promise new,
We rise with hope, a guiding light.
In every chant, our love rings true,
From shadows deep to heights of flight.

Communions of the Heart

In the stillness, our hearts align,
Silent echoes of love's embrace.
Each heartbeat a testament divine,
In whispers, we seek His grace.

With open hands, we share our dreams,
A sacred bond that will not break.
In love's pure light, our spirits gleam,
Together, every path we take.

Through trials faced, we lift our voice,
In songs of joy and hope renewed.
Each tear we shed, a sacred choice,
In communion, our strength is viewed.

As the sun sets, our prayers rise high,
Unfurling like wings, we take flight.
In every moment, we will not lie,
For love, dear friend, is our light.

With every gathering, hearts unite,
In reverence, our shadows cease.
Together we stand, in faith we fight,
In love's embrace, we find our peace.

A Sacred Symphony of Us

In the gentle dawn, we find our song,
A melody of grace and trust.
In harmony, we hum along,
With every note, our spirits gust.

Through valleys deep, and mountains high,
Our journey flows like rivers wide.
In sacred rhythms, we rely,
With love and faith as our guide.

The symphony of whispers pure,
Resounds beneath the open skies.
In sacred space, we feel secure,
With every breath, our bond complies.

When shadows fall, and doubts arise,
We lift our voices, strong and clear.
Together we rise, no compromise,
In unity, we persevere.

Thus, let the world hear our duet,
A harmony that will not fade.
In sacred notes, we won't forget,
The love within, forever laid.

Incantations of Intimacy

In the hush of dawn, we softly speak,
Incantations of love bestowed.
In the eyes we hold, truths unique,
A sacred path, forever flowed.

With every touch, a promise made,
In the quiet, our souls entwine.
Through shadows cast, we are unafraid,
In the warmth of love, we shine.

Every heartbeat, a sacred prayer,
Echoing through the realms of fate.
In intimacy, we lay bare,
The depths of love that won't abate.

As evening falls, our spirits rise,
In whispered breaths, our dreams unfurl.
With every glance, we synchronize,
Dancing in the sacred swirl.

With open hearts, we share our fears,
Through laughter, tears, and tender grace.
In incantations, love appears,
Forever cherished, in this space.

Celestial Murmurs of Belonging

In the quiet night we hear,
Whispers of the stars above,
Calling souls from far and near,
Binding hearts in sacred love.

Each droplet of the morning dew,
Holds a promise pure and bright,
A reminder, deep and true,
Of our bond within the light.

Footsteps on the path of grace,
Lead us to the well of lore,
In each glance, we find our place,
As we seek forevermore.

Voices rise in hymns of peace,
Uniting realms with every breath,
In this moment, fears release,
As we dance beyond our death.

Together, in this sacred space,
Hearts entwined in joy's embrace,
We find solace, love, and grace,
In celestial murmurs, we trace.

The Altar of Awareness

At dawn, we gather, souls aligned,
In the stillness of the morn,
With open hearts and eager minds,
We seek the truth that is reborn.

Each breath a prayer, each thought a vow,
Upon this altar, we reside,
With reverence, we humbly bow,
To the wisdom that does guide.

In silence, we find clarity,
In unity, we are made whole,
The essence of divinity,
Awakens deep within our soul.

In the flicker of the candlelight,
Our hopes ascend, our worries cease,
Together, we embrace the night,
Finding solace, joy, and peace.

And as we leave this hallowed space,
We carry forth what we have learned,
In every heart, a sacred trace,
Of love's eternal flame, discerned.

Seraphic Embrace of Essence

From realms unseen, the light descends,
Wrapping us in gentle grace,
In every heartbeat, love transcends,
A seraphic embrace we trace.

In the garden, blooms arise,
Each petal sings of what we share,
Underneath the vast starlit skies,
We find our truth in tender care.

With every tear that we release,
The burdens of our past dissolve,
In this moment, we find peace,
And through our pain, we are resolved.

Whispers of the angels soar,
Guiding us on paths unknown,
In this dance, we do explore,
The essence that we have outgrown.

As we gather, hand in hand,
Bound by love that never wanes,
In the embrace, we understand,
Together, we are whole again.

Pilgrimage of Hearts

We journey far on winding trails,
Seeking solace through the years,
With faith that never falters,
Our hopes alight with sacred tears.

Each step we take, a story told,
The stars above, our guiding light,
Through valleys deep and mountains bold,
We find our strength in darkest night.

In every prayer, a lift of soul,
Each voice a beacon, strong and loud,
Together, we become the whole,
A pilgrimage, joyous and proud.

With every dawn, we rise anew,
Older wisdom shapes our path,
Bringing forth the love we knew,
As we walk beneath the heavenly swath.

So here we stand, our hearts aflame,
In unity, we search and seek,
In every step, we share the same,
A yearning deep, both bold and meek.

Elysian Fields of Union

In fields where light shines bright,
Hearts unite in pure delight.
Hands entwined in sacred grace,
Together we shall find our place.

The whispering winds guide our way,
To lands where love shall ever stay.
Beneath the skies, painted gold,
In unity, our dreams unfold.

Each step we take, a prayer spoken,
A bond unyielding, never broken.
With faith, we walk this sacred ground,
In Elysian peace, we are found.

In the sun's embrace, we dance,
All souls together in blissful trance.
The melody of life resounds,
In harmony, our joy abounds.

Together we rise like morning's dew,
In every heartbeat, love shines through.
In Elysian fields, forever we roam,
With kindred spirits, we find our home.

The Dance of Kindred Souls

In twilight's embrace, we begin to sway,
Two souls aligned, as night breeds day.
With every step, our spirits soar,
In the dance of love, we crave for more.

The universe hums a celestial song,
While kindred hearts tap along.
In laughter and tears, our story we weave,
In each other's arms, we truly believe.

As stars twinkle in the vast expanse,
We celebrate life in this sacred dance.
Bound by the light that guides our way,
Together forever, come what may.

Through trials and joys, we hold each other near,
In the dance of souls, we conquer fear.
Every twirl is a prayer, every spin a vow,
With love as our guide, we're anchored now.

So let us dance, let our hearts ignite,
Under the moon's soft, silver light.
In this divine rhythm, we shall find,
The beauty of love, forever entwined.

Adoration in Every Teardrop

In the depths of sorrow, love still flows,
Each teardrop bears the weight of woes.
But in the pain, a beauty shines,
A silent prayer that intertwines.

For every tear, a story lives,
In moments lost, the heart forgives.
In sorrow's grip, we find our way,
Each drop a lesson, come what may.

With every sigh, the spirit grows,
In quiet strength, a hope bestows.
Adoration wraps around our fears,
Transforming pain into sacred years.

Through trials faced in soft embrace,
We mend our hearts, we find our place.
In every teardrop, love's gift unfolds,
A testament of faith in whispered holds.

So let the tears flow, let them cleanse,
For in each drop, our spirit mends.
With adoration, we rise anew,
Transcending the darkness, love shines through.

Celestial Paths Intertwined

In heavens above, our paths align,
Two souls destined, by stars designed.
In cosmic dance, we find our way,
Guided by light, through night and day.

Galaxies swirl in a rhythmic embrace,
Echoes of love in eternal grace.
Across the skies, our dreams take flight,
In the tapestry of timeless light.

Each moment shared, a spark divine,
In celestial realms, our spirits entwine.
With every heartbeat, the universe sighs,
As we chase our dreams beneath endless skies.

Together we wander, hand in hand,
Creating a world, tender and grand.
Through trials faced, our bond remains,
In love's sweet song, we break the chains.

So let the cosmos witness our love,
As we dance to the rhythm of stars above.
In celestial paths, we forever flow,
Intertwined in love, we'll always glow.

Guardians of Each Other's Souls

In the silence of the night,
We whisper prayers of light,
Bound by spirit, hand in hand,
Together we take our stand.

Through valleys deep, we tread with care,
With hearts unveiled, our burdens share,
A watchful gaze, a guiding hand,
Love's embrace, our sacred band.

In shadows cast by doubt's cruel veil,
We lift each other, we will not fail,
Anointed by grace, we rise as one,
The battle fought, the victory won.

Our souls entwined in sacred trust,
In gentle whispers, strong and just,
With every breath, we forge anew,
Eternal bonds, forever true.

Through the storms and sacred night,
Together we find the morning light,
As guardians of each heart's call,
We stand united, never fall.

The Sanctuary of Shared Dreams

In the quiet grove where wishes bloom,
We gather strength to conquer gloom,
A tapestry of hope we weave,
In the sanctuary we believe.

Each dream a star within our reach,
With hearts united, we will teach,
The power of faith, the art of grace,
In every tear, a warm embrace.

Bound by love, we speak as one,
A symphony 'til the day is done,
In the sacred space where we confide,
Together we grow, side by side.

The garden nurtured by our care,
Each seed a promise, rich and rare,
With every dawn, new visions rise,
In this sanctuary, hope never dies.

In deep communion, our spirits soar,
Guided by dreams, we seek for more,
With every heartbeat, pure and bright,
We share our dreams, we share our light.

Eternal Palm to Palm

In the stillness of the dawn,
We join our hands, we are reborn,
Palm to palm, our spirits greet,
In unity, we feel complete.

Across the miles, we bridge the gap,
With every prayer, we close the lap,
A bond unbroken, pure and strong,
Together we sing a sacred song.

In the temple of our hearts,
Love endures, never departs,
With gentle strength, we hold the line,
In every struggle, love will shine.

A circle formed of trust and grace,
With every challenge, we'll embrace,
In the heartbeat of our shared resolve,
In unity's dance, we evolve.

Through the trials that life may send,
Together we rise, we will not bend,
Eternal palms, a vision grand,
In love's embrace, we ever stand.

The Ritual of Endless Support

In the rhythm of the heart's deep beat,
We gather strength, we feel complete,
A ritual born of love's sweet grace,
In every smile, we find our place.

Through the trials that life may cast,
We hold each other, steadfast,
With open arms and listening hearts,
In every ending, a new start.

With whispered words and tender care,
We weave the tapestry we share,
A circle forged by faith and trust,
In every moment, we adjust.

In the dance of life, side by side,
Through joy and pain, we abide,
The ritual calls, we heed the song,
With every heartbeat, we grow strong.

In the sacred space where love is found,
We chant the truth, a sacred sound,
At the altar of our endless support,
Together we rise, our spirits court.

Epiphanies in Our Togetherness

In quiet moments, grace appears,
As whispered prayers dissolve our fears.
Upon our hearts, love's light descends,
Uniting souls, as one transcends.

In laughter shared, we find our way,
Through trials faced, we choose to stay.
In every tear, a joy is sewn,
For in your heart, I've found my home.

In sacred circles, bonds entwine,
Through every storm, your hand in mine.
Together, we create our song,
With every note, we grow more strong.

In sunlit fields, we dance as one,
While nature sings, our hearts are spun.
In simple acts of love, we bind,
A testament of the divine.

In visions shared, we seek the light,
In every dream, love takes its flight.
In unity, we shall abide,
Epiphanies, our hearts collide.

Hymns of the Truly Affectionate

In gentle whispers, love's refrain,
A melody that soothes all pain.
In sacred hymns, our voices rise,
As heartfelt truths, we harmonize.

With tender hands, we weave our fate,
In boundless love, we celebrate.
Each moment shared, a prayer takes flight,
In every heartbeat, pure delight.

In the stillness, spirits soar,
In unity, we seek for more.
Through trials fierce, our roots grow deep,
In love's embrace, our souls we keep.

In starry nights, our dreams ignite,
With hope as wings, we share the light.
Each word a balm, each glance divine,
In this great dance, hearts intertwine.

In every sorrow, joy's embrace,
In love's pure light, we find our grace.
With open hearts, we sing our song,
A hymn of love, where we belong.

Celestial Alignments of Hearts

In cosmic whispers, hearts align,
A dance of faith, a sacred sign.
In every gaze, a star is born,
As love unfolds, our spirits sworn.

In sacred stillness, we align,
Each moment shared, a divine design.
Through trials faced, we stand as one,
In endless night, we chase the sun.

In shared silence, the world fades away,
In mindful breaths, our spirits play.
Each heartbeat echoes, a sweet refrain,
In love's embrace, we'll break every chain.

In celestial paths, our souls entwine,
As whispers of love through space, they shine.
In unity, we soar through the skies,
A testament that never dies.

In every sunrise, hope is reborn,
In every dusk, our hearts are worn.
With every touch, a promise stays,
In celestial love, we find our ways.

The Testament of Fused Spirits

In sacred bonds, our spirits fuse,
Through trials faced, we're never loose.
In every heartbeat, love's decree,
A testament of you and me.

In gentle eyes, the truth is seen,
A love that flows, forever keen.
In joyful laughter, hands entwined,
In every moment, love defined.

In trials fierce, we stand as one,
Through darkest nights, we chase the sun.
In whispered prayers, our hopes abide,
With faith as our unyielding guide.

In acts of kindness, spirits grow,
In every tear, the river flows.
In soulful glances, joy ignites,
Our hearts united, reaching heights.

In timeless verses, love will speak,
In every vow, our spirits peak.
With every breath, a story shared,
In love's embrace, we are prepared.

Reverence in Simple Acts

In quiet prayer, we bend our knees,
With open hearts, our souls at ease.
In humble tasks, divine we find,
The holy glow, in love aligned.

The sunlit dawn, a sacred sign,
A gentle touch, a hand in mine.
In laughter shared, in tears we shed,
In every moment, love is fed.

With grateful hearts, we gather round,
In every smile, His grace is found.
A whispered word, a kindness shown,
In simple acts, His love is known.

The morning dew, a blessing rare,
In nature's song, we sense His care.
With open eyes, we see the light,
In every day, our spirits flight.

So let us walk with reverent grace,
In every time, in every place.
With love and faith, our hearts will sing,
In simple acts, we praise the King.

Emissaries of Elysium

We walk the path where angels tread,
With whispered prayers, our souls are fed.
In every step, we seek the sublime,
Emissaries of the holy rhyme.

In sacred woods, the spirits play,
Their laughter brightens every day.
In gentle winds, their voices glide,
With nature's grace, we bide our time.

Through trials faced, we hold the light,
In shadows deep, we reflect His might.
Anointed souls, we rise and soar,
In love's embrace, we seek for more.

Each kindly deed, a thread of gold,
In every heart, His love unfolds.
With hands extended, we reach wide,
As emissaries, we abide.

So let us weave the fabric strong,
Of unity, where we belong.
In harmony, our spirits mend,
To spread His word, our souls ascend.

The Blessing of Sacred Connection

In every gaze, a bond we share,
A glimpse of love, beyond compare.
In every heartbeat, a hymn of grace,
The blessing found in each embrace.

Through shared burdens, our hearts align,
In sacred moments, the stars will shine.
Each whispered prayer, a thread divine,
Connecting souls where love entwines.

The ties that bind, a holy thread,
In unity, our spirits fed.
With love like rivers, flowing free,
In sacred bonds, we truly see.

In laughter bright, in sorrows deep,
The love we share, forever keeps.
Through trials faced, we rise anew,
In sacred ties, our bond is true.

So let us cherish every look,
Each gentle word, our hearts the book.
In sacred connection, we find our way,
In love's embrace, we'll always stay.

Trysts Beneath the Stars

Beneath the stars, our spirits meet,
In whispered dreams, our hearts repeat.
With silver light, the night reveals,
The love that in the silence heals.

In sacred vows, we find our grace,
In every touch, a holy space.
As constellations shine above,
In night's embrace, we speak of love.

Through moonlit paths, we wander free,
In every glance, eternity.
With gentle words, our fears release,
In this great love, we find our peace.

With every heartbeat, time stands still,
A testament of God's sweet will.
In starlit skies, our dreams take flight,
A dance of souls, a pure delight.

So let us gather beneath the moon,
In sacred moments, hearts attune.
For in this dance, forever bound,
In love's embrace, true joy is found.

Fortresses of Emotion

In the chambers of the soul, we dwell,
Where whispers of faith weave a sacred spell.
Each tear a prayer, each laugh a hymn,
Building strong walls for love within.

In shadows cast by doubt's cruel hand,
We find our strength, we take a stand.
With every heartbeat, a promise renewed,
Fortresses rise where love is pursued.

Amidst the storm, our spirits soar,
Finding solace in the evermore.
Each fortress built on trust and grace,
A haven found in love's embrace.

Though tempests rage and trials bind,
We gather light, with hearts aligned.
Together we shield, we lift each other,
In these strongholds, we're sister and brother.

Fear may knock at the gates of night,
But fueled by faith, we stand to fight.
In the fortresses of emotion's dance,
We find our peace, we take our chance.

The Light of Shared Paths

In the twilight glow, our journeys meet,
Footsteps echo with a harmony sweet.
In every shared moment, a bond is spun,
Guided by grace, together as one.

Through valleys low and mountains tall,
We walk as one, answering the call.
With hearts aflame and spirits bright,
Illuminating the darkest night.

Hand in hand, we traverse the way,
Each laugh a beacon, each tear a ray.
In the tapestry of hope we weave,
The light of shared paths, we believe.

For every shadow that seeks to divide,
We rise united, with love as our guide.
In the unity formed through every stride,
The light of shared paths shall not subside.

Bound by faith, we journey forth,
Each step a testament of our worth.
Together in love, forever we roam,
In the light of shared paths, we find our home.

Prayers of Unspoken Promises

In silence, we speak, our hearts converse,
With whispers of hope, we break the curse.
Unseen vows in the stillness reside,
Prayers of promise we shall not hide.

Through trials faced and joys embraced,
The bond we share cannot be replaced.
In every heartbeat, a sacred trust,
With unspoken prayers, we know we must.

Beneath the stars, our dreams take flight,
In the quiet hours of the night.
Hands raised high, our spirits soar,
In prayers of unspoken promises, we explore.

Each moment cherished, each memory sealed,
In the garden of faith, our love revealed.
For every challenge, together we stand,
In unseen vows, we find our land.

So let us tread on this hallowed ground,
In the embrace of love, we've truly found.
With prayers lingering, we softly bless,
Unspoken promises, our souls' caress.

Sanctified Yearnings of the Heart

In the chorus of dawn, our spirits rise,
Yearning for light that never dies.
With every breathe, a sacred sigh,
Sanctified yearnings as time goes by.

In the depths where hope does dwell,
We seek the truth, the tales to tell.
With open hearts and hands raised high,
Sanctified dreams reach toward the sky.

Through every trial, we whisper grace,
In the fabric of love, we find our place.
The heart's desire sings soft and clear,
With sanctified yearnings, we hold dear.

On this journey where souls entwine,
We gather strength, in love divine.
In every yearning, a promise made,
In the echoes of faith, we won't be swayed.

So let us wander this sacred land,
With sanctified yearnings forever hand in hand.
Through valleys deep and mountains steep,
We hold our dreams, our hearts to keep.

The Lantern of Shared Paths

In twilight's grace our souls unite,
Each step we take, a path of light.
With faith as guide, hand in hand,
We walk together, a sacred band.

Through trials faced and joy we find,
The lanterns glow, our hearts aligned.
In whispers soft, we feel the glow,
Of love that leads where rivers flow.

In shadows deep, we seek the flame,
That lights our way, brings hope, no shame.
Companions true, we share the load,
With every bond, our spirits grow.

As stars above in night's embrace,
We Journey forth, in sacred space.
Each moment shared, a gift divine,
A tapestry of love entwined.

So let us walk this path of grace,
With open hearts, in love's embrace.
Together strong, we find the way,
With lanterns bright, we greet the day.

Rituals of the Heart's Truth

In silence sacred, whispers start,
The dance of souls, the truth of heart.
With every breath, we hold it dear,
A ritual of love draws near.

In sacred circles, hands entwined,
We seek the light, our spirits aligned.
With gentle words and open eyes,
We touch the heavens, hear the sighs.

In moments shared, we breathe as one,
The heart's great truth has just begun.
Through trials faced and laughter shared,
In rituals deep, our love is bared.

From whispered prayers to joyful song,
We feel the pulse where we belong.
With eyes like stars, reflecting grace,
In every heartbeat, we find our place.

So let us gather, let us sing,
In every heart, the joy we bring.
For love is the truth, forever free,
In rituals held, we come to be.

Echoes of the Beloved's Promise

In morning light, your voice I hear,
An echo sweet that draws me near.
With whispers soft upon the breeze,
You speak the love that brings me ease.

Through seasons change, your words remain,
A promise held, through joy and pain.
In every touch, in every smile,
The promise grows, through every mile.

In shadows cast by doubt and fear,
Your echoes call, I hold them dear.
With every heartbeat, I draw near,
For in your love, my path is clear.

As rivers flow and mountains stand,
Your promise lives, a guiding hand.
In every moment, in every prayer,
The echoes rise, love fills the air.

So let us dance beneath the stars,
With echoing love that heals our scars.
In every echo, in every sigh,
The beloved's promise will never die.

The Essence of United Spirits

In gentle silence, we align,
Two spirits strong, in love divine.
With every breath, our souls combine,
In harmony, we seek the sign.

Through trials faced and laughter shared,
The essence blooms, together bared.
In every glance, a world unfolds,
A sacred tale, our love retold.

With open hearts and arms so wide,
We find our strength, with love as guide.
In unity, we rise and soar,
For together, we can be much more.

From distant shores to skies above,
The essence speaks, a song of love.
In joy we find, in tears we heal,
The united spirits, forever real.

So let us walk this sacred path,
With every moment, feel love's wrath.
For in this essence, we are one,
The united spirits, ever spun.

A Testament to Togetherness

In the shadow of grace, we stand firm,
Hand in hand, through the storm we squirm.
With faith as our beacon, we rise and shine,
A testament to love, yours and mine.

Through trials met with a spirit so pure,
In the dance of the heart, we find our cure.
Each laugh and each prayer we share as one,
A journey of souls, forever begun.

The whispers of hope in the silent night,
Bind us together, our spirits ignite.
In moments of doubt, we lean, we trust,
For in unity's bond, we find our must.

With every sunrise, a promise to keep,
In the valley of kindness, our blessings reap.
Through the tapestry woven with light and care,
Together we flourish, together we dare.

For love is the thread that stitches our fate,
In this mosaic of faith, we congregate.
As the seasons unfold, our roots shall grow,
A testament of togetherness, we sow.

Audiance of the Heart

In the stillness of prayer, we gather near,
Voices rising softly, hearts sincere.
With each whispered thought, we touch the divine,
An audience of souls, in sacred design.

In silence we listen, the truths unfold,
Stories of faith in the warmth of the bold.
With every heartbeat, a echoing sound,
The rhythm of worship, in love we are found.

Through trials we speak, with courage and grace,
Together we journey, in this holy space.
In the embrace of the light, shadows pass,
The audience of the heart is forged, made to last.

Each moment we share, a precious embrace,
In the dance of the spirit, we find our place.
With hands intertwined, our burdens we bear,
An audience of hope, together in prayer.

For in this communion, we rise and we shine,
In the warmth of the spirit, our paths intertwine.
With joy, we are lifted, in love, we partake,
An audience of the heart, together we wake.

Enshrined in Every Touch

In every caress, a blessing is found,
In the grace of each moment, our ties abound.
With gentle intent, we weave love's embrace,
Enshrined in every touch, sacred space.

With eyes that reflect the light from above,
We nurture the bonds of unwavering love.
In laughter and pain, our hearts intertwine,
Through the tapestry of life, divine design.

Each gesture, a whisper of faith in the air,
In the softness of presence, we learn to care.
As hands clasp together, our spirits ignite,
Enshrined in every touch, we find our light.

With fervor, we gather, lost souls made whole,
In the beauty of togetherness, we reach our goal.
For in every embrace, a promise is made,
Enshrined, forever, in love's serenade.

Through the trials we bear and the joys that we share,
In the language of kindness, we sow and we dare.
With every heartbeat, our union holds much,
For we are enshrined in every loving touch.

The Language of the Devoted

In the hush of dawn, our spirits align,
With openness woven in hearts that entwine.
A language of love, both gentle and bold,
The devoted rise up, with stories retold.

Through prayer and deep silence, our souls do speak,
In the warmth of connection, we're strong when we're weak.
Each smile, each tear, a reflection of grace,
In the language of the devoted, we find our place.

With unity forged in the fires of trust,
In the beauty of surrender, we learn what is just.
With hands raised to heaven, we seek the divine,
The language of the devoted, a sacred design.

Through the echoes of ages, our voices unite,
In the dance of existence, we bask in the light.
For love is our language, pure and profound,
In the hearts of the devoted, true joy is found.

As time flows like rivers, our bond shall remain,
In the temple of spirit, we rise from the pain.
With every heartbeat, the truth we evoke,
For in the language of the devoted, we are awoke.

The Exquisite Divine

In the stillness of prayer's gentle embrace,
We seek the light that leads us to grace.
In whispers of faith, our spirits align,
Together we bask in the exquisite divine.

Each heartbeat echoes a sacred refrain,
Drawing us closer, through joy and through pain.
In shadows of trials, our love will refine,
Hand in hand, we trust the exquisite divine.

Moments of silence, our souls intertwined,
A tapestry woven, by love redefined.
From dawn's soft glow to the moon's silver sign,
We celebrate life, the exquisite divine.

With gratitude carved in the depths of our hearts,
In every new dawn, a fresh journey starts.
In the dance of the heavens, our souls brightly shine,
Forever embraced by the exquisite divine.

Symphony of Two Hearts

In the cradle of love, a melody grows,
Two hearts entwined, where compassion flows.
Notes of affection that sing through the night,
A symphony bright in the softest of light.

Through valleys of sorrow and mountains of joy,
Together we stand, no force can destroy.
In the rhythm of laughter, in solace we part,
Creating a masterpiece, the symphony of hearts.

Every challenge faced is a note in our song,
A chorus of hope where we both belong.
In the cadence of love, our fears we outsmart,
A harmonious journey, the symphony of hearts.

With every prayer whispered, our souls intertwine,
In unity soaring, our spirits align.
Wrapped in this music, both tender and stark,
We find our sweet refuge, the symphony of hearts.

Grace in Shared Harmony

In the quiet of dawn, our spirits awake,
Finding the path that our hearts will take.
With kindness as our guide, love's gentle decree,
We dance in a world full of grace, you and me.

Every moment together, a sacred embrace,
In laughter and tears, we find our place.
Through trials and triumphs, as time flows free,
We cherish the beauty, in shared harmony.

With faith as our anchor, we weather the storms,
In the warmth of belief, our hearts seek new forms.
As petals of blossoms, each day we foresee,
The gentle unfolding of grace in harmony.

In the tapestry woven, by love's tender art,
Lies the truth of our journey, a sacred counterpart.
Together we flourish, in perfect decree,
A testament living, of grace and harmony.

Soundings of Sacred Affection

Beneath the starlit sky, our hopes softly sing,
In the whispers of night, our souls take wing.
Each heartbeat resounding with love's pure reflection,
In the harmony blessed, soundings of affection.

With every gentle touch, the world fades away,
In the glow of your presence, I long for the day.
Through valleys of silence, and mountains of connection,
We echo the promise in soundings of affection.

Embracing the beauty found deep in our eyes,
In the depth of our laughter, our spirit can rise.
Through trials and triumphs, our hearts find direction,
Creating a symphony, soundings of affection.

Rooted in faith, through the shadows we dance,
In the light that you bring, there's a glorious chance.
Forever unbroken, this sacred reflection,
The sweetest of melodies, soundings of affection.

In the Temple of Affection

In sacred halls where love abides,
The whispers of the heart reside.
With every prayer, the spirit sings,
United, we embrace the wings.

Soft candles glow with tender might,
Each flame a promise, pure and bright.
In courtly silence, souls entwine,
A bond so deep, it feels divine.

In laughter shared and tears that fall,
We gather close to heed the call.
An altar built with trust and grace,
In this, our bliss, we find our place.

Through trials faced and victories won,
In harmony, we are as one.
With every heartbeat, love's refrain,
A sacred tune that will not wane.

In the temple of affection's glow,
The seeds of kindness gently sow.
Together, hand in hand, we stand,
In this, our promised, blessed land.

Celestial Bonds of the Soul

In the stillness of the night,
The stars align, a radiant sight.
A tapestry of love up high,
Threads of fate that twine and tie.

With every glance, a spark ignites,
Two souls connect in silent rites.
In heavenly realms, our spirits soar,
Bound together forevermore.

Through trials faced, our faith remains,
In whispered prayers, we ease the pains.
Celestial bonds that ever grow,
A light that guides, a heart aglow.

When shadows creep and doubts arise,
We lift our gaze, we touch the skies.
In unity, we find the way,
To embrace the dawn of every day.

With grateful hearts, we cherish grace,
In love's embrace, a sacred space.
In this communion, deeply whole,
We gather strength, the bonds of soul.

Reverent Echoes of Togetherness

In gentle whispers, hearts align,
Reverberate, our love divine.
In quiet moments, echoes play,
A symphony that guides our way.

In every heartbeat, rhythms blend,
Together we rise, ascend and mend.
Through trials shared, our courage grows,
In reverent echoes, love bestows.

With hands entwined, we forge ahead,
In sacred silence, words unsaid.
In harmony, our spirits dance,
Together, forever, lost in trance.

When darkness clouds the path we tread,
A beacon shines, where angels led.
With faith as our eternal guide,
In togetherness, we shall abide.

In every blessing, grace bestowed,
A testament of love, our ode.
In this embrace, forever blessed,
The echoes of our souls find rest.

The Prayer of Intimacy

In whispered prayers, our hearts converge,
In silent vows, our spirits surge.
A sanctuary built on trust,
In every moment, love's a must.

We delve deep into the sacred space,
With gentle touches, we find our place.
In eyes that speak, we learn to see,
The beauty that's in you and me.

Through tender nights and sunlit days,
We navigate life's winding ways.
In every heartbeat, faith ignites,
The prayer of love, a path of light.

In vulnerability, we lay bare,
Two souls entwined in honest prayer.
We cultivate the seeds of grace,
In intimacy, we find our place.

With hands held tight, we journey on,
Together, in the light of dawn.
In love's embrace, we are made whole,
The prayer of intimacy guides the soul.

The Art of Unspoken Devotion

In silence, hearts entwine with grace,
A sacred bond, a timeless space.
Through whispered prayers beyond the night,
We find our way, led by the light.

Beneath the stars, our spirits soar,
In every breath, we seek and implore.
A language forged in love's pure flame,
Devotion's art, unspoken, untamed.

In quiet moments, truth unfolds,
Secrets shared that cannot be told.
With humble hearts, we bow and kneel,
To feel the depth of what is real.

Through every trial, we stand as one,
In joy and sorrow, till life is done.
With gentle hands, we craft our fate,
In silent prayer, we resonate.

Eternal is this sacred trust,
Our souls entwined, in love we must.
In every heartbeat, a sacred song,
The art of love, where we belong.

Where Spirits Meet

In the quiet dusk where shadows play,
Our spirits gather, find their way.
A bridge of light, though worlds apart,
In every prayer, a beating heart.

Where sacred echoes softly call,
We rise together, never fall.
With open minds and arms that sway,
We greet the dawn of a new day.

In realms unseen, our souls take flight,
In unity, we embrace the night.
The whispers bind us, soft and clear,
In every moment, love draws near.

Where spirits dance in cosmic space,
We find our joy, a warm embrace.
With every step, a promise made,
In this union, fear shall fade.

Through timeless realms, our faith ignites,
A tapestry of shared delights.
In every heartbeat, truth reveals,
Where spirits meet, the heart then heals.

Unfolding the Divine Journey

Step by step, we walk this path,
With faith in hand, to feel the wrath.
Through trials faced, we learn to see,
The beauty in a life set free.

With open hearts, we seek the light,
In shadows deep, stars shine so bright.
Each moment holds a sacred chance,
To rise again, in love's sweet dance.

The road is long, but never worn,
With every dawn, a promise born.
Through sacred texts and whispered lore,
We find the truth, forevermore.

In every choice, a lesson learned,
With every flame, our spirits burned.
From doubts to faith, we forge our way,
In this divine unfolding, we sway.

Together we embrace the hour,
As life bestows its endless power.
In unity, we shall ascend,
A journey blessed, to never end.

The Vows of Affectionate Souls

In gentle vows, two souls face one,
In love's embrace, we are as one.
With every promise, hearts unite,
The stars align, our bond burns bright.

Through storms we weather, hand in hand,
In faith, we trust, on sacred land.
With laughter shared and tears made pure,
These vows we speak, forever sure.

In every glance, a story told,
In tender moments, warmth unfolds.
With whispered dreams, we craft our fate,
In love's soft glow, we resonate.

As seasons change and time moves fast,
With every breath, we hold on tight.
In unity, our spirits soar,
These affectionate vows, forevermore.

In every heartbeat, love we weave,
In life's embrace, we truly believe.
For every vow, a promise made,
In this holy bond, we are unafraid.

A Sacrament of Shared Moments

In whispers soft, the prayers arise,
Where two souls meet beneath the skies.
A bond of faith, like morning light,
In holy moments, hearts take flight.

Together in grace, we walk this path,
In joy and sorrow, we share the math.
Each fleeting glance, a sacred thread,
In love's embrace, our spirits wed.

With every laugh, a hymn we sing,
To sacred joys that friendship brings.
The tapestry of life we sew,
In every stitch, the blessings flow.

In silence shared, the soul's reply,
A trust that's forged, it cannot die.
Through trials faced, hand in hand,
Together we rise, together we stand.

The ritual of the everyday,
In simple acts, the divine does stay.
A sacrament, this life we weave,
In love's embrace, we truly believe.

When Hearts Speak the Divine

In the stillness, a heartbeat swells,
When spirits meet, the silence tells.
A sacred truth in whispers found,
Where two souls echo, love resounds.

With every glance, a prayer is sent,
In quietude, our hearts relent.
A language rich, beyond the words,
In gentle breath, the unseen stirs.

When hands entwine, the world stands still,
In acts of kindness, we bend our will.
The divine dwells in our embrace,
A holy touch, our hearts are grace.

Through trials fierce, together we fight,
In shared sorrows, we find the light.
The sacred dance of joy and pain,
In every moment, love we gain.

In harmony, our spirits sing,
The bond of faith, eternal spring.
When hearts unite, the angels sigh,
In the breath of oneness, we soar high.

Ceremonies of the Heart

In gatherings small, the sacred breath,
We honor life within the depths.
Each joyous laugh, a sacred song,
In ceremonies, we all belong.

The ritual of sharing bread and wine,
In fellowship, our spirits align.
With open hearts and hands held tight,
We find our way through darkest night.

From dawn to dusk, we mark the days,
In every moment, love's embrace stays.
The sacred pulse of life unfolds,
In unity, our hearts grow bold.

With every story, a lesson learned,
The fires of hope within us burned.
In laughter shared and tears that flow,
Our sacred bond continues to grow.

In every season, the heart does lead,
In ceremonies, we plant the seed.
Together in love, we find our place,
In sacred moments, there is grace.

The Pilgrim's Embrace

With steady feet upon the way,
A journey long, we choose to stay.
In every step, the earth we trace,
In pilgrims' hearts, we find our space.

Through valleys deep and mountains high,
We seek the truth beneath the sky.
With open arms, we face the dawn,
In every moment, we move on.

The path may twist, the road may bend,
In every trial, our spirits mend.
Together, we tread on sacred ground,
In love's embrace, our peace is found.

In every face, a story told,
In shared embraces, hearts unfold.
A pilgrimage of the soul's delight,
In every shadow, we find the light.

As we walk forth, hand in hand,
We weave our dreams across the land.
In every hug, the world ignites,
In the pilgrim's love, our hope ignites.

Chronicles of the Devoted

In whispered prayers we tread the night,
With faith as our guiding light.
Hearts entwined in sacred grace,
Seeking solace in Christ's embrace.

Through trials faced, our spirits soar,
With every drop, we crave for more.
In unity, our voices rise,
Worshipping beneath the skies.

The echoes of love, they softly plead,
In trials faced, we plant the seed.
From ashes born, rebirth and glow,
A garden where sweet blessings flow.

With hands uplifted, reaching high,
In the stillness, we hear the cry.
For every tear that falls in prayer,
A promise made, we know He's there.

As chronicles unfold, we stand side by side,
In God's embrace, we will abide.
Through valleys low and mountains grand,
Our journeys meet, our souls expand.

Halo of Heartstrings

Beneath the stars, our spirits twine,
A halo glowing, pure divine.
In harmony, our voices sing,
The joy that faith and love can bring.

With every heartbeat, we echo grace,
In sacred rhythms, we find our place.
Together bound, in love's grand scheme,
A tapestry spun from heaven's dream.

Each prayer we weave, a thread of gold,
In quiet whispers, our truths unfold.
With hearts aglow, we mark our way,
In unity, we greet the day.

For hope is found within each soul,
A lingering light that makes us whole.
In faith we walk, hand in hand,
With love's embrace, forever we stand.

The halo shines, our guiding star,
Reminding us just who we are.
In every moment, let love reign,
As heartstrings pull, we break the chain.

Embrace Within the Sanctuary

In sacred halls, where echoes dwell,
We gather close, our stories tell.
With open hearts, we find our peace,
In loving arms, our fears release.

The sanctuary hums with grace,
In every smile, a warm embrace.
With gentle hands, we lift each other,
In bonds of faith, we're sister, brother.

Through whispered hopes and shared belief,
We seek to heal with sweet relief.
In solace found, our spirits rise,
Bathed in light, beneath wide skies.

Together we walk this sacred ground,
In love's pure whisper, we are found.
With every verse, a hymn we sing,
In the sanctuary, our hearts take wing.

Embraced by faith, we conquer strife,
In unity, we celebrate life.
As one we stand, with hands held tight,
In the sanctuary of purest light.

Hymns of the Boundless

In fields of gold, our voices rise,
A hymn of love beneath the skies.
In every note, a story played,
Of grace bestowed and debts repaid.

With hearts unchained, we break the mold,
In every truth, our faith grows bold.
The boundless skies echo our song,
In love's embrace, where we belong.

Each step we take, a choice divine,
Guided by love, our hearts align.
In every breath, a prayer we make,
With every sacrifice, our hearts awake.

As songs of hope fill the air,
In sacred rhythms, we find our share.
Together we stand, in joy we sing,
Of all the blessings that love can bring.

So let us share this boundless grace,
In every smile, in every trace.
Our hymns will echo through the years,
In love's embrace, we dry our tears.

Prayers Under the Shared Stars

Beneath the vast and twinkling sky,
We gather hands, our spirits high.
In whispers soft, our hopes ascend,
Each prayer a message, love to send.

The night enfolds our yearning hearts,
Where every dream and wish imparts.
Through cosmic light, our voices soar,
In unity, we seek much more.

Stars witness all, our faith combined,
Each gleaming dot, a prayer aligned.
Together, we embrace the night,
As souls entwined, we share the light.

With every breath, a sacred vow,
To cherish each, to live the now.
In silence deep, our thoughts converse,
A sacred space, we freely traverse.

In harmony, the worlds collide,
As love and grace, our guiding tide.
Through prayers shared, our hearts ignite,
Beneath the stars, our souls take flight.

Cascading Blessings of Togetherness

In the garden of our souls we stand,
Holding tightly to each other's hand.
A river of joy, it flows so free,
With every heartbeat, you're part of me.

From the mountains high to valleys low,
Together we bloom, together we grow.
In laughter's echo, in tears that fall,
Each moment shared, we rise, we call.

The sun's embrace warms our weary fears,
In the dance of time, we share our years.
Through trials faced, with love we mend,
Cascading blessings that never end.

In twilight's hush, our spirits blend,
Each heartbeat echoes, we comprehend.
A tapestry woven with threads divine,
In every color, you're truly mine.

Hand in hand, we forge our fate,
A bond unbroken, we celebrate.
In every dawn, our hopes emerge,
With cascading blessings, we shall surge.

Sacred Whispers of the Heart

In the stillness of the night, we find,
Sacred whispers, gentle and kind.
Voices echo in the quiet air,
Speaking truths we all can share.

From depths of silence, love takes flight,
Guiding our spirits toward the light.
In every muffled sigh and dream,
We discover unity, a stream.

In the shadows, where hearts align,
A sacred bond, so pure, divine.
Each heartbeat's rhythm, a song so sweet,
In whispers soft, our souls entreat.

With courage found, we seek the way,
Through sacred truths that brightly sway.
Our deepest fears begin to part,
In the sacred whispers of the heart.

Together we walk on this life path,
Balanced in love, we embrace the math.
With every breath, we create anew,
In sacred whispers, I find you.

From dawn to dusk, our spirits sing,
In every moment, joy we bring.
With every whisper, united we start,
In the sacred space of every heart.

Divine Threads of Connection

In the fabric of life, our threads entwine,
Stitched by grace, so pure, divine.
A tapestry woven with love and care,
In every stitch, our spirits share.

Through trials faced and joys embraced,
In moments fleeting, our truths are traced.
Divine connections, strong and bright,
Illuminating even the darkest night.

Each tear and smile, a pattern spun,
In this grand design, we are one.
With hearts aligned, we seek to find,
The sacred union of heart and mind.

With every prayer, new threads unite,
In sacred spaces, we shine so bright.
Through laughter shared and burdens eased,
The ties we forge, forever seized.

In the silence that binds, we stand tall,
In the dance of life, we hear the call.
With every heartbeat, love's reflection,
In this sacred web, our connection.

Through every challenge, we shall prevail,
With divine threads, we cannot fail.
Together, we find life's sweet perfection,
In this journey, our divine connection.

The Guardian of Sacred Affection

In shadows cast by love's soft grace,
A guardian stands with a warm embrace.
Through trials faced and storms that blow,
In sacred light, true hearts shall grow.

With whispers sweet of hope divine,
They guide the lost, their souls entwined.
In every tear and laughter's song,
The guardian's spirit makes us strong.

Through every path that life may take,
Their gentle touch helps our hearts awake.
In unity found, our faith endures,
For in this bond, love's heart assures.

The sacred bond, a timeless thread,
In every prayer that we have said.
When shadows creep and doubts arise,
The guardian shines, forever wise.

Through ages past and days ahead,
With sacred affection, we are led.
In every journey, through joy and strife,
The guardian blooms, the breath of life.

Illuminated Footprints on the Earth

Each step we take, a tale unfolds,
In golden light, the truth retold.
With every footprint on this ground,
A sacred path of grace is found.

Illuminated by spirit's glow,
In love's embrace, we learn and grow.
Through trials faced and lessons learned,
With faith ablaze, our hearts are burned.

The earth beneath, a canvas wide,
Of stories shared, with love our guide.
Each soul a star in heaven's grace,
With illuminated steps, we trace.

Together we weave a tapestry bright,
A journey of souls in shared delight.
With every stride and whispered prayer,
Illuminated, we conquer despair.

In twilight realms where shadows play,
Hope shines forth, guiding our way.
With every footprint, echoes stay,
In sacred love, we find our way.

The Mirror of Kindred Spirits

In reflections deep, our spirits meet,
A mirror held, where hearts compete.
With tender grace, our souls align,
In kindred unity, love divine.

Each laugh and tear, a echo shared,
In mirrored depths, we are prepared.
The bonds we forge in silent nights,
Reveal the truths in shared delights.

As seasons change and embers fade,
The mirror shines, our love conveyed.
In every glance, in every sigh,
Our spirits dance, we learn to fly.

In sacred spaces filled with light,
Together we conquer the longest night.
A tapestry of dreams and fears,
Reflected love across the years.

In every moment, hearts entwined,
The mirror whispers, love defined.
In kindred spirits, bound by fate,
In love's embrace, we mediate.

Wings of Connected Souls

Like gentle breezes, we rise and soar,
With wings of love, we seek to explore.
In the heart of silence, whispers roam,
Connected souls find their way home.

Through skies of dreams and fields of light,
With wings that lift our spirits bright.
In every heartbeat, love takes flight,
Bound by the sacred, day and night.

In every challenge, we find our grace,
Two souls entwined in a warm embrace.
With every journey, new heights we reach,
In connection's glow, our hearts teach.

Love flows freely like rivers wide,
With wings unfurled, we cast aside pride.
Together we rise, fearless and bold,
In harmony written, our stories told.

With every breath, our spirits sing,
In love's embrace, we find our wings.
Connected as one, through joy and pain,
With wings of hope, we shall remain.

The Alchemy of Shared Souls

In the whispering night, we stand as one,
Hearts beating softly, under the same sun.
Each gaze a promise, transcending time,
Together we're sacred, in rhythm and rhyme.

Through trials and triumph, our spirits blend,
In the dance of existence, we find the mend.
Hand in hand onward, through shadows we tread,
With faith as our anchor, our paths gently spread.

Voices united, in prayer we rise,
Holding the heavens, beneath sacred skies.
In laughter and struggle, our union is pure,
With love as our light, forever we endure.

In silence we listen, to truths held dear,
The warmth of our bonds casts away all fear.
As seasons are woven, in time's gentle weave,
We find in each other, the grace to believe.

Two souls intertwined, like vines they ascend,
In the garden of love, where all hearts can mend.
Through the alchemy shared, our essence ignites,
A divine celebration, in ethereal flights.

Spirit's Embrace in the Ordinary

In the mundane moments, divinity calls,
With each gentle breath, the spirit enthralls.
A smile exchanged, a touch so divine,
In daily encounters, the sacred aligns.

In the rustle of leaves, in the morning light,
We find the holy, in simplicity's sight.
Every cup of kindness, every shared glance,
Is a whisper of heaven, in life's fleeting dance.

The warmth of a hug, the song of the breeze,
We meet in the ordinary, drifting with ease.
Gratitude flows, like a river so deep,
In each fleeting moment, the spirit we keep.

Hand in hand walking, on paths made of grace,
In laughter and tears, we find our true place.
Every heartbeat echoes, a love ever true,
In the embrace of the spirit, I'm awakened with you.

A gentle reminder, in the still of the night,
The sacred is here, in the ordinary's light.
With open hearts, we unveil love's disguise,
In the fabric of life, the divine ever lies.

Beneath the Veil of Companionship

In the hush of the dawn, two souls convene,
Beneath the veil of trust, a love evergreen.
With whispers of hope, our spirits entwined,
Together we flourish, in the light we find.

In laughter and silence, our hearts softly sing,
Beneath the cloak of friendship, blessings take wing.
With every shared secret, every tear shed,
We unearth the depths where our fears have fled.

With each passing moment, our bond's grown profound,
In the sanctuary of love, true grace is found.
As petals of time fall, we cradle each change,
In the circle of solace, we rise and exchange.

Through valleys of shadow and mountains of light,
The compass of friendship guides us through the night.
In the warmth of connection, our spirits ignite,
With faith in the journey, our visions take flight.

Wrapped in the whispers of shared memories dear,
Beneath the veil of togetherness, love is near.
In communion we flourish, on this sacred ground,
With each heartbeat resonating, forever we're bound.

The Divine Caress of Intimacy

In the stillness of night, our hearts intertwine,
A whisper of love, in each sacred sign.
With breath held in wonder, we tread on soft ground,
In the caress of intimacy, our souls are unbound.

Gentle embraces, like the waves of the sea,
In the depth of our bond, we find harmony.
Every shared moment, a treasure to hold,
In the light of our union, we daringly unfold.

In the dance of our laughter, as stars softly gleam,
We find in each other, the essence of dream.
With eyes locked in knowing, we glimpse the divine,
In the weave of our hearts, no boundary defines.

Hand in hand walking, through shadows and light,
The divine caress guides us, a beacon so bright.
In the depth of our silence, the world fades away,
For here in this moment, love's promise will stay.

Through the trials and laughter, we're bound ever tight,
In the sanctuary built from intimacy's light.
With every heartbeat, our spirits ascend,
In the sacred embrace, love knows no end.

Milton Keynes UK
Ingram Content Group UK Ltd.
UKHW020039271124
451585UK00012B/937